D0793332

TROON HARRISON

The BIRDMAN

Illustrated by

FRANÇOIS THISDALE

Red Deer Press

Published in Canada by Red Deer Press
195 Allstate Parkway, Markham, ON L3R 4T8

Published in the United States by Red Deer Press
311 Washington Street, Brighton, MA 02135

www.reddeerpress.com

10 9 8 7 6 5 4 3 2 1

Library and Archives Canada Cataloguing in Publication

Harrison, Troon, 1958-, author
The birdman / Troon Harrison ; illustrated by François Thisdale. – First edition.

ISBN 978-0-88995-506-6 (hardcover)

1. Ross, Alexander Milton, 1832-1897–Juvenile fiction. 2. Ornithologists–
Canada–Juvenile fiction. 3. Underground Railroad–Juvenile fiction. 4. Fugitive
slaves–Juvenile fiction. I. Thisdale, François, 1964-, illustrator II. Title.

PS8565.A6587B57 2018   jC813'.54   C2018-903965-5

Publisher Cataloging-in-Publication Data (U.S)
Names: Harrison, Troon, author. | Thisdale, François, 1964-, illustrator.
Title: The Birdman / Troon Harrison ; illustrated by François Thisdale.
Description: Markham, Ontario : Red Deer Press, 2019. | Summary: "The story of
Alexander Milton Ross, Canadian ornithologist and undercover Abolitionist,
who helped spread word among enslaved men and women in the American South
about the Underground Railroad" – Provided by publisher.
Identifiers: ISBN 978-0-88995-506-6 (hardcover)
Subjects: LCSH: Ross, Alexander Milton, 1832-1897 –Juvenile literature. | Abolitionists—
Biography – Juvenile literature. | Underground Railroad – Juvenile literature. | BISAC: JUVENILE
NONFICTION / Biography & Autobiography / Historical. | JUVENILE NONFICTION /
History / Canada / Pre-Confederation (to 1867).
Classification: LCC E449.R67H377 |DDC 326.8092 – dc23

Red Deer Press acknowledges with thanks the Canada Council for the Arts and the Ontario Arts
Council for their support of our publishing program. We acknowledge the financial support of the
Government of Canada through the Canada Book Fund (CBF) for our publishing activities.

Edited for the Press by Peter Carver
Cover and interior design by Kong Njo

Printed in China by Scheck Wah Tong Printing

For Anne, Lynn, and Sue;
dear friends through thick and thin

– T.H.

To my friend Martine

– F.T.

William and Frederika's baby was born on December 13, 1832.
Winter gripped the hills and woods of Upper Canada, and snow
covered the town of Belleville where the baby lay snug in his
cradle. Frost coated the logs in the lumber mill, and ice reached
into the gray waves of Lake Ontario. William and Frederika
named their new-born Alexander Milton Ross.

When spring came, Frederika carried her baby outside to
see birds returning and green buds swelling on maple trees.
She held petals of wood anemone to his cheeks and tickled
him with coltsfoot flowers.

As Alexander grew into a sturdy child, spring continued to be a special time for him and his mother.

"Let's go to the woods!" he cried, tugging at her arm. Laughing, she laid down her needlework and picked up her straw hat. Together they roamed woods, swamps, fields, and the shoreline of Lake Ontario.

Frederika taught Alexander the names of everything he touched and smelled. When he saw a bright orange flash overhead, he asked, "What is it?" and his mother said, "It's an oriole." When he heard a sweet noise, he peered into the treetops. "What is singing?" he asked. "It's a thrasher," his mother replied, pointing to a bird with a speckled breast and long tail.

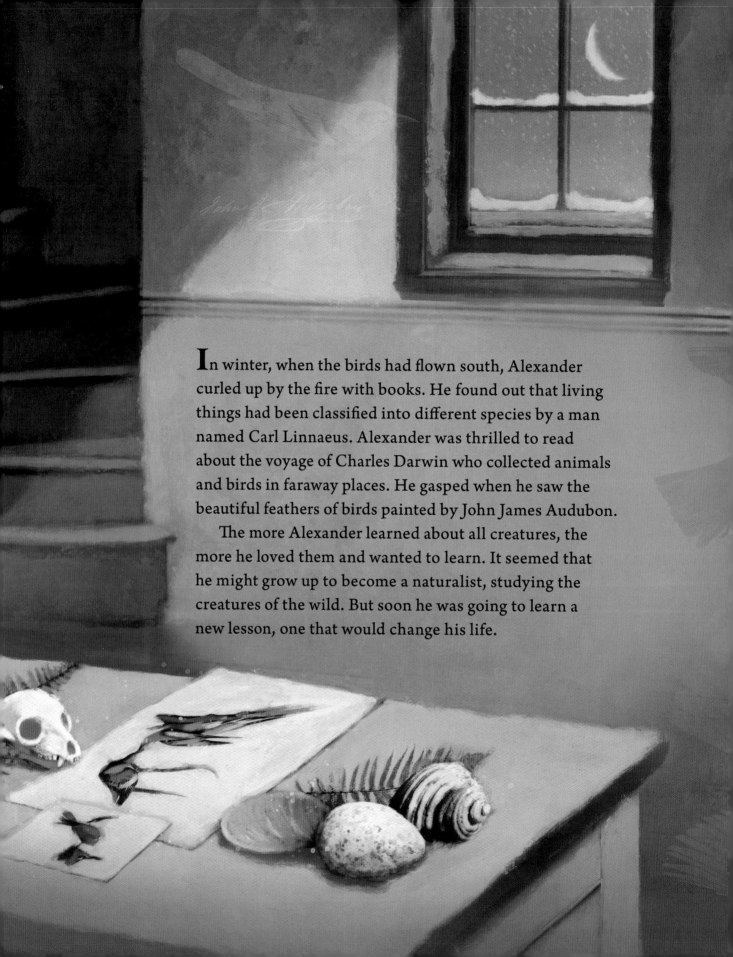

In winter, when the birds had flown south, Alexander curled up by the fire with books. He found out that living things had been classified into different species by a man named Carl Linnaeus. Alexander was thrilled to read about the voyage of Charles Darwin who collected animals and birds in faraway places. He gasped when he saw the beautiful feathers of birds painted by John James Audubon.

The more Alexander learned about all creatures, the more he loved them and wanted to learn. It seemed that he might grow up to become a naturalist, studying the creatures of the wild. But soon he was going to learn a new lesson, one that would change his life.

One day, a group of exhausted people climbed from a merchant ship onto the wall of Belleville harbour. They were escaping slaves who had crossed the lake, from the United States to Upper Canada. Although the ship had been bound for Toronto, a storm had blown it off course. Alexander's father felt sympathy for the bedraggled group. "Come home with me and rest," he urged.

Frederika gave a cry of surprise when the front door opened. "You must eat before you journey on!" she said. "Please, come and sit in the parlor." She brought the freedom seekers food on her best china. Alexander and his parents listened as their guests told stories of their escape.

One former slave slipped off his shirt. Alexander touched the ridged scars from a cruel whipping. He stared as his mother used warm salt water to clean a woman's leg, bitten by bloodhounds. Another woman had a knotted red scar on her cheek. Her cruel master had burned his own initials there with a hot iron.

The travelers needed to journey on to Toronto to find work. "Alexander, take our new friends to the lumberyard," said William. "They can hitch a ride westwards on a wagonload of boards."

Alexander shoved his feet into his boots and strode beside the slaves. It was hard to imagine that they had walked so far on their bare feet. He felt deep admiration for their determination and courage.

As they crossed the Moira River's wooden bridge, the slaves stared curiously around. "Look at that bird!" cried the woman with the brand. "That bird done live on my master's plantation in Alabama!" Alexander tilted his face as the bluebird soared high.

"That bird done fly all the way north," said the man. "It more free than my wife and children left behind in Mississippi."

Alexander never forgot the suffering he saw in the eyes of those former slaves. He thought about how a bird could fly free but a person could be bought and sold, beaten, and whipped. He pondered his mother's words: "Live by the Golden Rule, my son. Treat others in the same way that you want to be treated."

Alexander continued tramping around outdoors, sketching lady's slipper orchids and marsh hawks in flight. Indoors, he listened as his father read aloud the words of men, including George Washington and Thomas Jefferson, who were interested in equality for all people.

Alexander's mother wasn't a writer but she had plenty to say. "The most worthy ambition is to alleviate people's suffering," she told Alexander. "You need to leave the world some better than you found it."

Alexander realized that every person had a right to freedom. He itched to do something good in the world, something great that would change things. But what could he do? He was only a young boy from a small backwoods town with one schoolhouse.

In 1844, when Alexander was twelve years old, William died. Now the Ross home was filled with grief, and the boy had no father to help him choose an education or find work.

If Alexander hoped to do something good in the world, he would have to figure it out on his own.

Alexander grew into a tall young man with wide shoulders. When he was seventeen, he decided it was time to become independent. His mother gave him the name of a family friend in New York City and Alexander traveled there to start his adult life. He worked as a printer's devil in a newspaper office by day. But he had not forgotten his dream and in the evenings he studied to become a doctor.

In the city, Alexander met many people called abolitionists, who did not believe in slavery. They took big risks to help slaves escape north to freedom. People called the escape route the Underground Railroad. Alexander wanted to help with this work. People warned him it was very dangerous. In many states, anyone helping to free slaves could be whipped, sent to prison, or hanged.

Late at night, after his studies, Alexander read a new book about the cruelty of slavery. *Uncle Tom's Cabin* started a fire burning in his heart. From now on, he decided to use all his energy to helping slaves reach freedom.

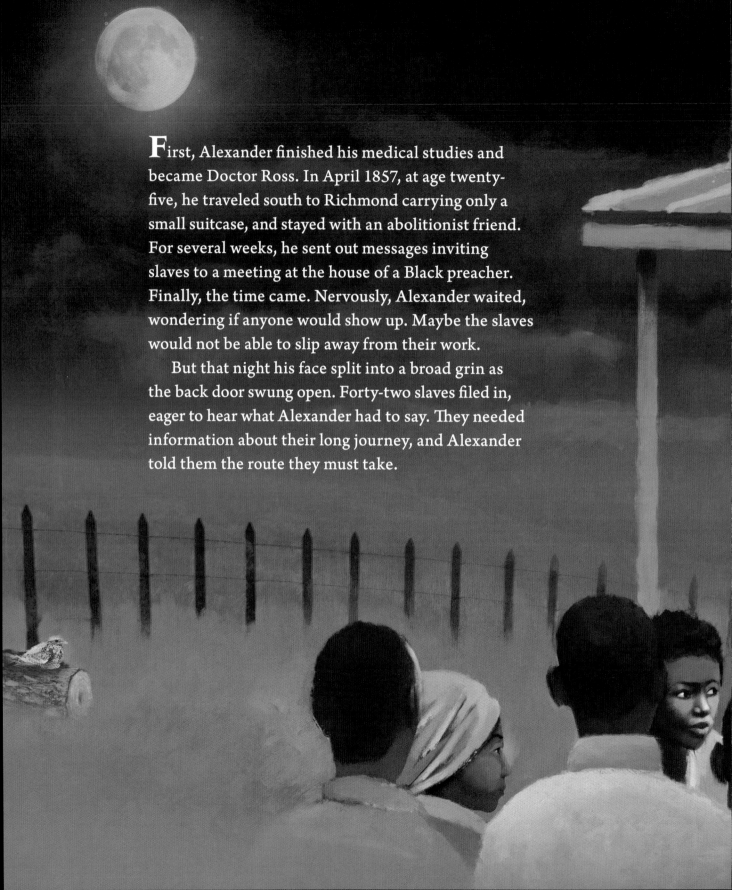

First, Alexander finished his medical studies and became Doctor Ross. In April 1857, at age twenty-five, he traveled south to Richmond carrying only a small suitcase, and stayed with an abolitionist friend. For several weeks, he sent out messages inviting slaves to a meeting at the house of a Black preacher. Finally, the time came. Nervously, Alexander waited, wondering if anyone would show up. Maybe the slaves would not be able to slip away from their work.

But that night his face split into a broad grin as the back door swung open. Forty-two slaves filed in, eager to hear what Alexander had to say. They needed information about their long journey, and Alexander told them the route they must take.

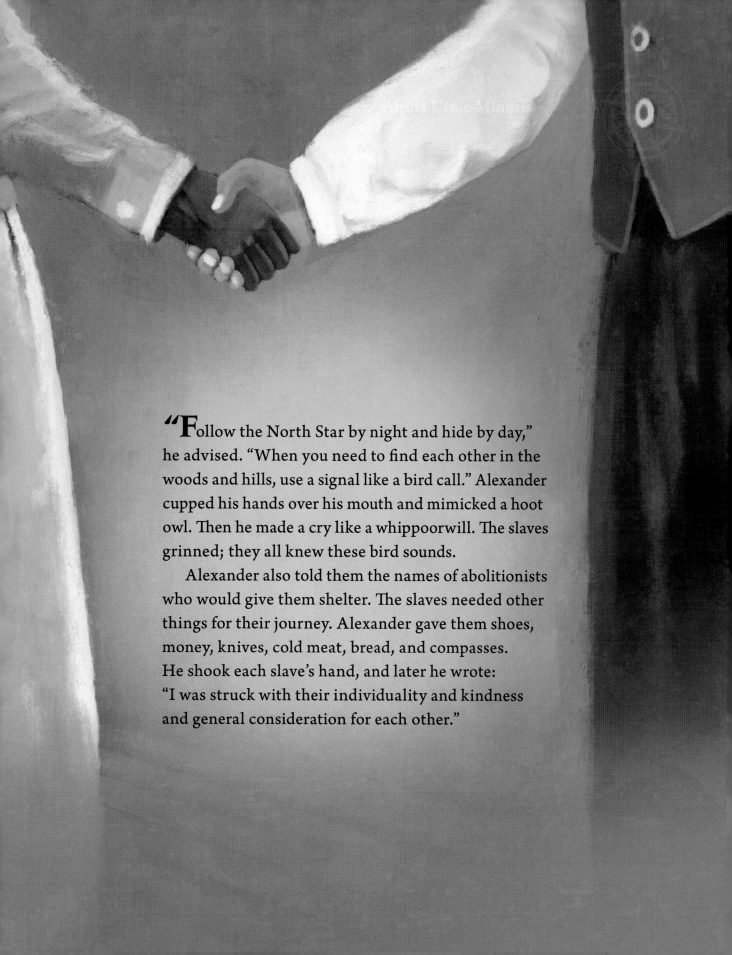

"Follow the North Star by night and hide by day," he advised. "When you need to find each other in the woods and hills, use a signal like a bird call." Alexander cupped his hands over his mouth and mimicked a hoot owl. Then he made a cry like a whippoorwill. The slaves grinned; they all knew these bird sounds.

Alexander also told them the names of abolitionists who would give them shelter. The slaves needed other things for their journey. Alexander gave them shoes, money, knives, cold meat, bread, and compasses. He shook each slave's hand, and later he wrote: "I was struck with their individuality and kindness and general consideration for each other."

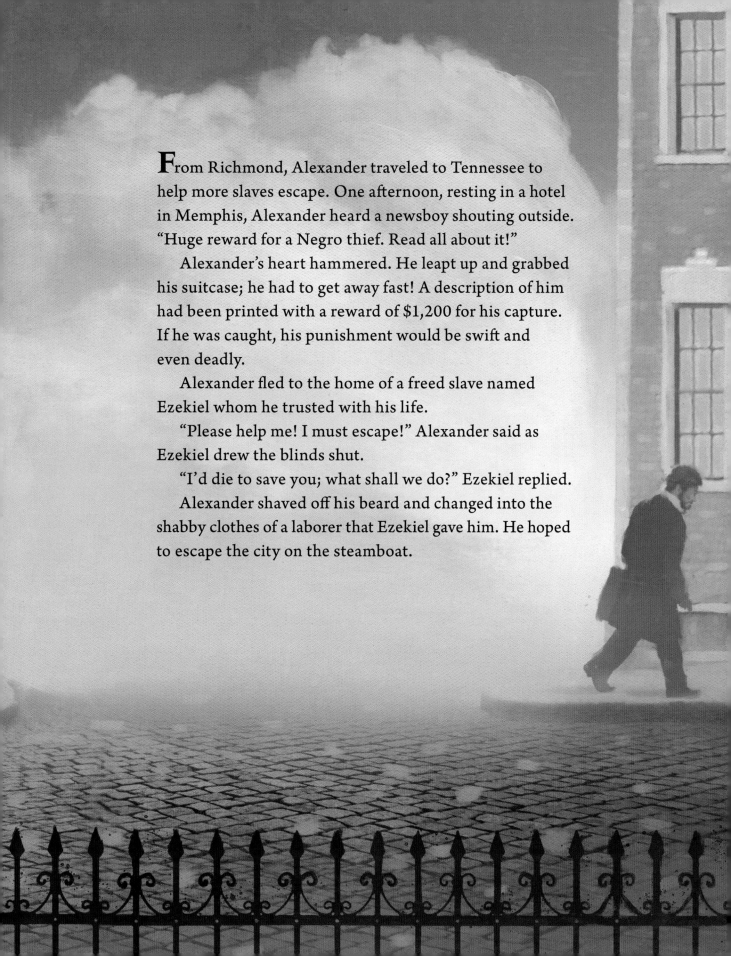

From Richmond, Alexander traveled to Tennessee to help more slaves escape. One afternoon, resting in a hotel in Memphis, Alexander heard a newsboy shouting outside. "Huge reward for a Negro thief. Read all about it!"

Alexander's heart hammered. He leapt up and grabbed his suitcase; he had to get away fast! A description of him had been printed with a reward of $1,200 for his capture. If he was caught, his punishment would be swift and even deadly.

Alexander fled to the home of a freed slave named Ezekiel whom he trusted with his life.

"Please help me! I must escape!" Alexander said as Ezekiel drew the blinds shut.

"I'd die to save you; what shall we do?" Ezekiel replied.

Alexander shaved off his beard and changed into the shabby clothes of a laborer that Ezekiel gave him. He hoped to escape the city on the steamboat.

Suddenly, someone beat frantically on the front door. Ezekiel peeked out. When he opened the door, a woman rushed inside, gasping. Blood trickled through her ripped dress. "Help me!" she begged. "My husband done escape to Canada last week. Now my massa be trying to make me marry someone else. When I refuse, he have me whipped!"

Alexander disguised the woman as a man and named her Sam. Together they escaped on the steamboat with Sam pretending to be Alexander's servant. "Massa, is we near heaven yet?" Sam kept asking. Heaven was what many slaves called Canada. Fear and dread filled Alexander on this long journey by boat and horse carriage, but finally the two travelers reached the Detroit River.

In the darkness, a friend rowed Alexander and Sam to the safety of Windsor, Canada. Alexander breathed a deep sigh of relief. Now he knew exactly how frightened the slaves were as they fled north. Years later, Alexander visited the woman and her husband who had bought their own house in London, Ontario.

Alexander planned another trip to help slaves, this time in Alabama and Mississippi. He thought up a clever way to keep himself safe. On his travels in 1858 he took along a shotgun and some arsenic, a chemical used to preserve bird skins. Many people were interested in collecting and classifying birds, mammals, and insects. The dead, preserved specimens were used for museum collections.

"Sir, I am interested in studying the bird species of this state," Doctor Ross told wealthy plantation owners. "May I have permission to roam in your cotton and tobacco fields, collecting specimens?" Usually, the owners agreed.

And so Alexander collected and preserved many different species of birds. Sometimes, he saw his old favorites flying overhead: the bright orioles and sweetly-singing thrashers. He remembered his mother teaching him their names. She had also taught him about making the world a better place. Once he glimpsed a bluebird and thought how it was free to fly wherever it chose.

Alexander wasn't only thinking about birds. Working as an ornithologist, he was able to talk secretly to the field slaves. They told him about being beaten with paddles, slashed with bull whips, and chained together.

"We suffer death many times before we die," one woman said. "And we always hungry; we just eat ground corn and no meat."

"We be so wore out, even our bones ache," said another woman. "We go stumbling to the fields before dawn, after the bell rings and wakes us."

"Slavery be the wickedes' curse on this earth," summed up a bent old man. "When we find grubs in the crops, we got to bite off their heads with our own teeth!"

Alexander told all the slaves he met about the Underground Railroad. When the overseers' backs were turned, he slipped them money and knives. He drew maps for them in the dirt. He taught them to memorize the names of friends who would help them reach freedom. At night the slaves talked around their fires. They spread the news about walking north. Alexander had a new name: the slaves called him The Birdman.

One evening in Mississippi in 1858, Dr. Ross was arrested for helping a slave escape from his owner. Alexander's wrists were shackled in iron. Curses and shouts filled the hotel where he had been eating dinner. "Hang him!" shouted people in the crowd.

After a miserable night in a jail filled with rats, Alexander was marched before a judge. Cold, tired, and hungry, he waited for punishment. It's hopeless, he thought. Many people think that no mercy should be shown to abolitionists, the people who help slaves to escape.

"Here is Joe!" shouted a voice outside. The door was flung open. In rushed the slave whom Alexander had helped to escape. Kneeling before his master, Joe explained that he had gone to visit his brother, and sprained his ankle walking back. He asked his master for forgiveness for being late in returning. Hearing this, the judge let Alexander go.

The truth was that Joe had started to flee north. When he heard about Alexander's arrest, he gave up his freedom so he could return and save Alexander. Later, Joe and his brother tried again and escaped safely.

In 1860, Alexander traveled in Kentucky. On a farm that was for sale, he met a slave named Peter who had just married another slave. Peter loved Polly very much but they belonged to different masters. "When my massa done sold the farm," Peter told Alexander, "he plan to take me away with him to Texas. He ain't taking Polly. I ain't never going to see my good wife again." Tears rolled down Peter's face.

Alexander went to stay at the hotel where Polly worked. He whispered quickly to her at the kitchen door. "Peter is going to run away and you can escape too. Sneak out at midnight and meet me at the post office."

"I'm scared," Polly said, gripping the dirty plates.

"Just promise me," said Alexander, before going to make the arrangements. At midnight, they met and sneaked to the Ohio River where a friend waited to row them across.

They traveled to Cincinnati by horse cab, then on foot. Peter arrived safely, his feet torn and sore from his long walk. He and Polly were reunited with cries of joy. Alexander arranged for them to be shipped north in boxes. The boxes were loaded into a freight train rumbling to Cleveland. With a friend, Alexander met the train and freed Peter and Polly from their cramped boxes. Then he whisked them into a carriage and drove to the docks where they boarded a schooner.

After midnight, the wind rose and the sails were hoisted. All night and the next day, the ship pitched across the lake until it reached Canada. Polly and Peter fell to their knees and kissed the ground; they were together and they were free. Watching them, Dr. Alexander Ross smiled. He understood what his mother meant when she said, "You need to leave the world some better than you found it."

The escaped slaves would surely agree that their lives were made better by Alexander's courage. Alexander liked to think that the children and grandchildren and all the descendants of those slaves would have better lives too. Meanwhile, he knew that there were still many things for him to do in his own lifetime. He would keep on loving nature and loving freedom.

Historical Notes

From my mother I received a heritage of qualities which have been ruling factors in my labours for the betterment of humanity—a love of nature, and a love of freedom.

Dr. Alexander Milton Ross wrote these words in his book, *Memoirs of a Reformer.* Public service was another tradition Alexander learned from his family. On his mother's side, his great-grandfather had been Governor of Rhode Island from 1727 to 1732. On his father's side, his great-grandfather had been a captain in the army of General James Wolfe in the battle over Quebec.

Alexander's parents believed in liberty and equality for all humans. Although slavery was not legal in Canada in the early 1800's it was still practised in the southern United States. Thousands of slaves, helped by abolitionists, traveled north to Canada on the Underground Railroad where they began new lives. Escaped slaves were always welcome in the home of Alexander's parents.

While he was studying medicine in New York City, Alexander began a life-long friendship with the famous Italian freedom fighter, Giuseppe Garibaldi, as well as with many abolitionists and Quakers. Ross dedicated four years of his life to traveling throughout the southern U.S. giving assistance to slaves. This work was treasonous under the law of many states, and Dr. Ross' capture could have been punished with jail or hanging. He also risked his medical career, as being an abolitionist was an occupation that many people despised. American Senator Benjamin Wade wrote that no abolitionist "submitted to greater privations, perils or sacrifices, or did more in the great and noble work than Alexander Ross." The Quaker poet, John Greenleaf Whittier, wrote a poem in which he praised Ross' "steadfast strength and courage." After his work to help many slaves to escape, Alexander later visited with some of them in Chatham, Upper Canada, which was one of the northern termini of the Underground Railroad.

After the election of President Abraham Lincoln, Dr. Ross worked in Canada as an undercover agent and special correspondent for Lincoln. His task was to spy and report on the activities of Confederate plotters. Lincoln credited Ross with helping to hasten the end of the American Civil War.

When slavery was outlawed in the United States, Ross was free to focus his energy on his passion for the natural world. He was the first Canadian to attempt to collect and classify all of the country's flora and fauna. He wrote and had published numerous books about the plants and animals of Canada, and collected a vast array of specimens: 570 species of migratory birds, 247 species of mammals, reptiles, and fish; 2,200 species of plants, and 3,400 species of insects. He sent many specimens to natural history collections in Europe, including those in Rome, Paris,

St. Petersburg, Athens, Lisbon, Tehran, and Vienna, and he was a member of various organizations including the British Association of Science, the Linnaean and Zoological Society of England, and the Imperial Society of Naturalists of Russia. He was awarded many honours during these years, including knighthoods from the Emperor of Russia, and the kings of Italy, Greece, Portugal, and Saxony.

Ross was also appointed to the Canadian consulate in Belgium and Denmark, and held the position of Ontario Treasurer and Commissioner of Agriculture. He led a crusade against vaccinations in the Montreal smallpox epidemic, for vaccines were still a new science and the inconsistent quality of the serum used in them could pose health risks. Throughout his life, Ross was a vegetarian who believed in the benefits of drinking clean water and breathing fresh air. He crusaded in Montreal for improved municipal sanitation so that everyone could access pure drinking water, and he worked to educate people about healthy diets and clean living conditions. Ross and his wife Hester had five children, three of whom survived infancy, and raised them in Toronto.

A tall, strong, robust man, Dr. Ross brought great energy to all his passions. He corresponded with many famous men of his period including John Brown, who tried to raise troops in a fight against slavery in Virginia. This attempt was unsuccessful and John Brown was captured and executed. Another correspondent was the writer and philosopher, Ralph Waldo Emerson. Dr. Ross was influenced by many great thinkers of his day (including President Thomas Jefferson) and by the Victorian pursuit of studying the natural world. With his wide knowledge of philosophy, politics, abolitionism, medical advancements, and the flora and fauna of Canada, he was a Renaissance man from a small village in Upper Canada.

Alexander Ross died in Detroit on October 27, 1897.

TIME LINE

1707 – 1778 Linnaeus develops classification of species (published 1758)

1793 First anti-slavery legislation passes in Upper Canada, forbidding importation of any slaves into the province and freeing twenty-year old offspring of slaves

1807 Guiseppe Garibaldi born

1809 Charles Darwin born

1811 Harriet Beecher Stowe born

1832 Alexander Milton Ross born in Belleville, Ontario

1833 Formation of American Anti-slavery Society

1834 British Parliament abolishes slavery throughout its Empire, liberating 200,000 slaves

1841 British American Institute forms near Chatham, Upper Canada, then Dawn Settlement follows with mills, a school, and 200 acres of farms for former slaves

1844 Ross's father dies

1849 Ross, age seventeen, goes to New York to work in print shop, meets Guiseppe Garibaldi

1850 Fugitive Slave Law passes in America, making it treason to help any escaping slaves

1851 Ross begins studying medicine by night and works in printing shop of the *Evening Post* newspaper by day. This paper was owned by the poet William Cullen Bryant whose friendship enabled Ross to meet abolitionists and politicians.

1852 *Uncle Tom's Cabin* by Harriet Beecher Stowe is published

1854 Ross reads *Uncle Tom's Cabin*

1855 Ross, age twenty-three, graduates with his M.D. His mother dies.

1856 to 1859 Ross in active work as an abolitionist

1857 Ross marries Hester F. Harrington

1858 John Brown calls a meeting in Chatham

1859 Charles Darwin's *Origin of Species* published

1859 Harper's Ferry raid, John Brown executed

1861 American Civil war begins

1860's Ross collecting specimens of plants, insects, birds, fish, and mammals

1860 Abraham Lincoln elected President of United States of America

1863 President Lincoln issues the Emancipation Proclamation, abolishing slavery in the Confederate States

1864 President Lincoln's Emancipation Bill passes

1864 Ross works as President Lincoln's secret agent in Canada during the Civil War

1865 Ross and Hester settle in Toronto, the Civil War ends; slavery is outlawed by the Thirteenth Amendment to the American Constitution

1867 Ross receives an M.A.

1867 Ross publishes *Recollections of an Abolitionist*

1872 Ross is made a member, Royal Society of Literature, UK

1872 Ross made a fellow, British Assoc. of Advancement of Science

1872 Ross publishes *Birds of Canada*

1873 Ross publishes *Butterflies and Moths* as well as *Flora of Canada*

1874 Ross publishes *Forest Trees*

1874 Ross is made a fellow of the Linnaean Society of London

1875 Ross becomes a practising physician in Ontario

1876 Ross knighted in Russia

1877 Ross publishes *Ferns*

1878 Ross publishes *Mammals, Reptiles and Fish*

Up to 1881 Other international honours bestowed on Ross; he corresponds with Emerson, is made a Canadian Consul to Belgium and Denmark, is awarded medals in Italy, Greece and Portugal, and holds a position as Ontario Treasurer and Commissioner of Agriculture. He is knighted by the kings of Italy, Greece, Portugal, and Saxony, and by the Shah of Persia and the Emporor of Russia in recognition of his contributions to natural history.

1882 Garibaldi dies, and Darwin dies

1883 Ross publishes his *Memoirs* which he wrote for his children when he turned fifty years old

1885 Smallpox in Montreal

1896 Harriet Beecher Stowe dies

1897 Alexander Ross dies in Detroit

Notes on Sources of Visual Materials

Bibliography for The Birdman

Blight, David W, edited, *Passages To Freedom: The Underground Railroad in History and Memory*, Smithsonian Books 2004

Drew, Benjamin, *The Refugee: Narratives of Fugitive Slaves in Canada*, Dundurn Press, Toronto, 2008

Landon, Fred, "A Daring Canadian Abolitionist" *Michigan History Magazine* 1921, page 364

Ross, Alexander Milton:

    Butterflies and Moths of Canada

    Canadian Ferns and Wildflowers, Toronto 1873

    Memoirs of a Reformer 1832-1892, Hunter, Rose and Company, Toronto, 1893

    Recollections and Experiences of an Abolitionist From 1855 until 1865, Rowsell and Hutchinson, Toronto, 1875

    The Flora of Canada

    The Birds of Canada, Henry Rowsell, Toronto 1871

    Forest Trees of Canada, Rowsell and Hutchison, Toronto 1875

    Catalogue of the Mammals, Birds, Reptiles and Fishes of the Dominion of Canada, Montreal

Sadlier, Rosemary, *The Kids Book of Black Canadian History*, Kids can Press, Toronto, 2003

Smucker, Barbara, *Underground to Canada*. Originally published in 1977 by Clarke Irwin, Toronto. New edition by Penguin Books, 2013.

Switala, William J., *Underground Railroad in Delaware, Maryland and West Virginia*, Stackpole Books 2004

Tobin, Jacqueline, *From Midnight to Dawn: The Last Tracks of the Underground Railroad*, Doubleday, New York, 2007